THE LAST MISSION TANKER

WALTER W.
JAFFEE

This shot was taken November 10, 1943 while the Mission Purisima *was on sea trials in San Francisco Bay. Her sister, the* Mission Santa Ynez *presented the same clean, powerful lines on her sea trials.*

San Francisco Maritime National Historical Park

THE LAST MISSION TANKER

WALTER W. JAFFEE

To the men and women of the Marinship Corporation who made it all possible.

Original Copyright 1990 Walter W. Jaffee
Registration number 415-738, May 2, 1990

Second Edition, September, 1995
Library of Congress Catalog Card Number: 95-79380
ISBN 0-9637586-5-9

All rights reserved. No part of this book may be used or reproduced, stored in a retrieval system, or transmitted in any form or by any means, electronic, mechanical, photocopying or recording, or otherwise in any manner whatsoever without written permission except in the case of brief quotations embodied in critical articles or reviews.

PRINTED IN CANADA

Table of Contents

About the Author	6
Acknowledgements	7
The Mission Sisters	11
War Mission	31
Missions of Peace	45
Missions in Pieces	61
The Final Mission	75
Bibliography	78
Index of Ships	79

About the Author

Captain Jaffee received his Bachelor's degree in maritime transportation from the U.S. Merchant Marine Academy, Kings Point, New York, in 1965, and his master's license in 1970. In 1989 he received a master's degree in public administration from California State University, Hayward. He has sailed as a licensed deck officer in the merchant marine. Traveling the oceans many times, he has visited just about every country that touches water. For several years he was involved in operating a sportfishing and whalewatching business, and helped pioneer whalewatching in Northern California. He is currently employed by the Maritime Administration as Superintendent of the Suisun Bay Reserve Fleet.

His stories and non-fiction have been accepted by the following publications: *Air California Magazine, Aloft, American Boating, The American Journal of Nursing, The American Way, Captain Publications, The Compass, The Daily Press, Discovery, Ford Times, The Lookout, National Business Woman, The National Wildlife Federation, Naval Institute Proceedings, The Nautical Magazine, Oceans, Odyssey, Our Navy, Passages, Playboy, Ports O'Call, POSH, Salt Water Sportsman, San Francisco Magazine, The San Jose Mercury-News, Sea Classics, Sea Letter, The Student, USAir, Westways, The Yacht, Yachtsman* and *Young World.*

Many individuals and organizations were helpful in researching this book. Captain Ted Anderson, Captain Robert A. Bryan, Fred Splinter, Tony Sciavonne, the Marinship Museum, The staff of the J. Porter Shaw Maritime Library, Cindy Roby, Steve Haller, Shelley Rose, Bill Kooiman, Vic Young and Len Sawyer.

"There is witchery in the sea, its songs and stories, and in the mere sight of a ship …"

R.H. Dana, Jr.

Bow View Hull 32 Way 1, September 24, 1943, 15 days after keel.
Just 15 days after keel laying, the vessel already has the shape of a ship.
Courtesy National Maritime Museum, San Francisco.

1
THE MISSION SISTERS

Some ships, like some people, lead charmed lives. Fate serves up challenges that are handled with competence and grace. Such ships capture the imagination by their presence and their deeds. Their stories are told and embellished until they become legend. Other ships, like other people, struggle through life hampered by fate. All their contacts seem to be with "klutzes" who constantly make things difficult. When they are touched by competence, it is wasted. Their fate seems predetermined and they cannot change it. Such ships go from launch to break-up doing their best without fame or glory yet somehow muddling through. What, then, of these ships? What are the trials and triumphs, which make the life of an ordinary ship?

Even before the United States entered World War II, plans were made toward creating the much-needed tonnage to bolster our maritime strength. The U.S. Maritime Commission contracted with shipbuilding yards across the country for the construction of cargo ships. With our entry into the conflict, the timetable accelerated. At first ships were sunk faster than they could be built. Attempts at preventing the sinkings failed, so the goal became to build them faster than they could be sunk. Old, slow methods of plate by plate riveted construction were replaced by mass-production, prefabrication and welding.

In California, the W.A. Bechtel Co. agreed in March 1942 to create a shipbuilding facility in Marin County. The new company, known as the Marin Shipbuilding Division or the Marinship Corporation, promised to complete three EC-2 (emergency cargo) Liberty ships by the end of the year and an additional thirty-four by the close of 1943. Choosing the former site of the Northwestern Pacific Railroad's terminal in Sausalito, six shipways and their support buildings were constructed so rapidly that the first keel was laid just three months later, on June 27.

Captain Ted Anderson, wartime master of the *Mission Santa Ynez* remembered the Marinship yard in those days as an area of perpetual activity. People came from all over the country to work twenty-four hours a day building tankers. Marin City sprung up in a welter of temporary housing. "... all over the hillside back in there. The demographics of the entire United States got shifted all around.

"When the war first started the unions tried to slow these guys down. But I know up in the Todd yard in Seattle ... I had a friend that went to work there as a welder and the union said, 'hey, you can't do this. You're gonna ... you got a new standard for welding and we're not gonna have it.' And he quit and he said 'the hell with it. We're gonna be in a war effort and turn out a day's job.'"

In the spring of 1942, Germany launched a hard offensive against tanker traffic on the East Coast and in the Caribbean. The Maritime Commission notified many shipyards, including Marinship, to begin conversion to tanker construction. Marinship responded with such alacrity that the first tanker keel was laid on December 7, 1942, before drawings were completed or many materials ordered. Seventy-eight tankers were built in the following two years and ten months, and a world's record for tanker construction (thirty-three days) was set.

The basic tanker design proposed by the Maritime Commission was the T-2. A handsome design, it consisted of a three-island type hull with raked stem and modified cruiser stern. It was to tankers what the Model "T" Ford was to the automobile. A good, "no frills", easy-to-construct ship, it was serviceable and did what it was designed to do. To paraphrase Henry Ford, the customer could have it in any color he wanted as long as it was grey. The basic design was the T2-SE-A1. Powered by a 6000 horsepower engine, it was the prototype for what followed. There were modifications. A series of Navy oilers based on the T-2 design was built to Navy specifications.

A secondary design was the "Mission" tanker, named after the Catholic missions established in California in the late 18th and early 19th centuries. Officially known as the T2-SE-A2, each vessel in this class was powered with a 10,000 horsepower turbo-electric engine. The bigger engine pushed the fully loaded ship along at 16 knots versus 14.5 for the standard T-2. Armament consisted of one 5-inch 38, one 3-inch 50, and eight 20mm mounts.

Bow View Hull 32 Way 1, October 29, 1943, 50 days after keel.
Fifty days after keel laying, the bow and bridge begin to take shape.
Courtesy National Maritime Museum, San Francisco.

Ted Anderson remembered the Mission tankers as being difficult for the engineers.

"... from the standpoint of breakdown and the necessity for repairs, I'll tell you they were just absolute workhorses for engineers. They were terrible, just terrible. The big problem with those Mission ships though, more than the standard T-2 with the 6000 horsepower plant, was you had a higher pressure and higher temperature on those boilers. Those darn handhold plugs on the economizer element had what they called a flexitallic gasket on them and they were what you might say a bastard gasket that was part metal and part asbestos. They'd wind up leaking and steam would come out and cut a groove in the steel or the seat of the gasket. They (Mission tankers) almost became, you might say, something you'd stay off of.

"Another thing that we played with all the time was condenser leaks. They didn't have this copper-nickel tubing at the time. I forget what kind of tubing it was, but you were constantly dumping sawdust into the condensers to plug up all these holes. And then every once in a while you just had to stop and then you replaced the tubes in those condensers. And that seemed to be more of a problem in the Mission ships."

Number thirty-two in this series of tankers was the *Mission Santa Ynez*. Named after the Franciscan Mission established 40 miles northwest of Santa Barbara, she was hull number 32 for the Marinship yard. The keel was laid on September 9, 1943. Just 101 days later, on December 19th, she was launched.

Wartime launchings, although brief, were packed with pride and fanfare. Invitations for this one went out on December 11th. On Sunday the 19th the launching party gathered at 8 a.m. in Mr. Kenneth Bechtel's office just outside the shipyard proper. At 8:15 they walked to the launching way, with the ceremony beginning at 8:30. Taking their seats, those attending were awed by the massive ship, its bow towering above them. Were it an earlier age, the prow might have carried a figurehead. Instead it was adorned with a brightly colored "bow painting." In keeping with the season, the painting for this launching depicted Santa Claus. The ship and the yard were festooned with colorful signal flags and bunting.

Among those in the front row were R.W. Adams, the Marinship Employee Relations Manager, Chaplain Mortimer Chester, a Lt. Col. in the Army, K.K. Bechtel, President of Marinship, Ralph K. Davies, Deputy Administrator, Office of Petroleum Administration for War, his wife, Louise who was also the sponsor, Maryon Davies, the maid of honor, and Harold R. Bolton, chief

Bow View Hull 32 Way 1, November 26, 1943, 78 days after keel.

By day 78 the vessel looks more complete: anchor windlass, gun tubs, bitts and cargo tank accesses.

Courtesy National Maritime Museum, San Francisco.

Louise Davies, just after she launched the Mission Santa Ynez.
Courtesy Marinship Museum.

U. S. MARITIME COMMISSION TANKER
S. S. MISSION SANTA YNEZ

THIRTY-SECOND SHIP LAUNCHED BY
MARINSHIP CORPORATION
SAUSALITO, CALIFORNIA

Keel laid on September 9, 1943 Launched on December 19, 1943
Total time from keel laying to launching: 101 days

SPONSOR MAID OF HONOR
MRS. RALPH K. DAVIES MISS MARYON DAVIES

LAUNCHING PROGRAM
8:30 A. M., SUNDAY, DEC. 19, 1943

Welcome	R. W. ADAMS, Employee Relations Manager, Marinship Corporation
"O, Holy Night"	Marin Junior College Choir, CLINTON LEWIS, Director
Raising of the Flag	Members of Packs 36 and 41, Cubs, Boy Scouts of America, of San Francisco
"The Star-Spangled Banner"	Led by Marin Junior College Choir
Invocation	CHAPLAIN MORTIMER CHESTER, Lt. Col., U. S. Army
Introduction of Honored Guests	K. K. BECHTEL, Pres., Marinship Corporation
Remarks	RALPH K. DAVIES, Deputy Administrator, Office of Petroleum Administrator for War
Introduction of Maid of Honor and Sponsor	MR. BECHTEL
Response	MRS. RALPH K. DAVIES, Sponsor
Launching Procedure	Explained by HAROLD B. BOLTON, Chief Engineer, Marinship Corporation

Launching of the S. S. MISSION SANTA YNEZ, 9:00 A. M.

•

MISSION SANTA INES (Mission of St. Agnes Virgin and Martyr) was founded on September 17, 1804, in lovely Santa Ynez Valley by Fathers Tapis and Cipres, about forty miles northwest of Mission Santa Barbara. Its first buildings were destroyed in an earthquake in 1812, but new ones arose to meet the needs of a growing ministry. Now largely reconstructed, the beautiful campanile and chapel are regularly used for divine services.

Bow View Hull 32 Dock D-1, December 24, 1943, 5 Days After Launching.
Five days after launching the bow painting is still intact.
Courtesy National Maritime Museum, San Francisco

engineer for Marinship. Included with the other 85 guests were representatives of the Bechtel company, a number of oil companies and Father Celestian Quinlan, Padre of *Mission Santa Ynez.*

The ceremony started with a welcome by Mr. Adams. He was followed by the Marin Junior College Choir which sang "O, Holy Night." Members of Packs 36 and 41 of the Cub Scouts of San Francisco then raised the American flag as the choir sang "The Star-Spangled Banner." Chaplain Chester then gave a brief invocation, after which Mr. Bechtel introduced the guests. His first introduction was Father Quinlan.

Louise Davies: "I remember there was a father from one of the missions, I don't recall his name. Well of course he was from the Mission the ship was named after. And he was quite a friendly fellow and wanted to know what to say. I had no idea what he should say, and told him so. But he got through it with a prayer for the occasion and did rather nicely I thought."

Kenneth Bechtel then introduced Ralph Davies. "Some time ago an outstanding oil company executive from California went to Washington to lend his great talents in his country's service. He became Deputy Administrator. He carries a tremendous load in our war program because the direction of petroleum affairs is his responsibility. So Marinship, building tankers to carry oil for the Allied war program is very happy to welcome Mr. Ralph K. Davies, Deputy Administrator of the Office of Petroleum Administration for War."

After the applause, Mr. Davies responded. "America now is building vitally needed oil tankers ten times faster than the enemy can sink them. Somewhat over a year ago our tankers were being sunk ten times faster then we could build them. Had this rate of net loss continued many more weeks we would have been paralyzed. Planes, tanks and ships are so much junk without oil.

"The tide turned in America's favor in November 1942 after the United States Navy successfully combated the enemy submarine menace and American shipyard workers and operators began setting magnificent records."

Attention now focused on the ship resting tentatively in the launching cradle. All that held it was one final piece of steel awaiting the burner's torch. With Mrs. Davies in position, champagne bottle poised, the cutting began. At the right moment, just as the cut was complete, the Chief Engineer nodded. Louise Davies sent the bottle crashing against the ship's bow. With white champagne foam sparkling in the morning sunlight the great ship slowly began sliding, then gained momentum moving faster and faster like a great grey monster out of control until the stern splashed into the water sending waves radiating across the bay. The ship's motion continued until bight after bight of anchor chain tied off in loops on either bow broke the manila line holding it, the force of each snap slowing the vessel. Finally she stopped and the waiting tugs tied on, moving her rapidly to the finishing berth.

Flowers were presented to the launching party: a large corsage of orchids to Mrs. Davies, a smaller one to the Maid of Honor, corsages of bovardia to the youngest daughters and bouquets of American Beauty roses to the sponsor and Maryon Davies. They were then escorted to breakfast at the yard's facilities. Dignitaries dined at the exclusive Redwood Room while the remainder of the guests ate at the cafeteria. One's status determined where one ate. According to a note in the Marinship files:

> D.H.
> Mr. Adams would like you to include the choral group as guests to the Redwood Room to breakfast — not the cafeteria as there is a distinction and there might be some hard feelings. pn

The Redwood Room menu consisted of fruit juice, scrambled eggs, bacon, hot biscuits, corn bread, jam, coffee and milk.

Fitting out the vessel took almost as long as her construction, although the teething problems of the first Mission tankers which took over 200 days to complete, were well in hand. The builder's trials were held on Sunday, March 5, 1944. This was the opportunity for Marinship to find any last minute problems before declaring the ship fit and ready for use.

Beginning at 0748 the main engine was exercised by running it slow ahead and slow astern while the ship was still tied to the dock. Designed to give the engineers the opportunity to make sure the plant operated properly, these first tentative tests lasted until 1340 that afternoon.

The following day the ship was on her own for the first time. All lines were in by 0700 as the *Mission Santa Ynez* cleared the dock. Her initial moves were hesitant, even cautious, like those of an infant learning to walk.

At 0733 the port anchor was dropped in 75 fathoms of water. The next two hours were spent testing the anchor windlass. After weighing the anchors the final time, the steering gear was tested. In this operation the rudder is turned from hard over port to hard over starboard several times. This was followed by "swinging" the vessel, turning it in a circle, to allow for adjustment of the

Bow View Hull 32 Dock C, January 28, 1944, 40 days after launching.
Forty days after launching the externals are almost complete, but the myriad internal systems have a long way to go.
Courtesy National Maritime Museum, San Francisco.

magnetic compasses. As frequently happens, more than one circle was necessary. Although tedious, such maneuvering allows the compass adjuster to correct for the magnetism in the ship's steel hull.

By 1316 that afternoon the ship was running a speed trial, going full ahead across San Francisco Bay. A problem developed in the engineroom, the engine lost vacuum and the cargo pumps (which were being tested) were shut off. After anchoring the pumps were started again but had to be shut off once more. By 2300 that night the entire plant was shut down due to the main and auxiliary condensers being flooded.

By working all night the problems were resolved. The next morning the *Santa Ynez* was able to make another speed trial which included a crash stop and ahead and astern steering tests. Preparations were then made for the more formal "official" trial.

The Official Trial took place on March 11. This differed from the builders trial in that representatives of government regulatory agencies and the new owners (the Maritime Commission) were on board. The trial began ominously with engine problems. From the log:

0430 Slow ahead. Running lights on.
0433 Stop engine room.
     Engine room gave slow ahead.
0438 Engine room stop & slow ahead.
0453 Stop engine again, engine trouble.
     (Tug) Pacific forward taking line — started towing.
0455 Slow ahead. Stop again — waiting for engine room.
     Both tugs under bow towing out through channel.
0510 Slow ahead & stop.
0528 Slow ahead & stop, calling from engine room
     engine ready.

T-2s were intimidating ships. Not everyone could handle them.

Captain Anderson: "There was one fellow, his name was Schmidt and they called him Snuffy Smith. They sent him up to Portland at the time I took the *Corvallis* out of there as chief mate. He was a little guy and they assigned him as chief engineer. And he walked into this engineroom, and at that time the T-2 tanker was the largest tanker in the world. This massive switchboard was overpowering. He had a nabit when he got nervous of unbuckling his belt and stroking in his shirt-tails. And he stood up there on the upper grating and he looked down on this engineroom and went through this gyration and then walked out. He says, 'I'm going

Bow View Hull 32 Dock C, February 25, 1944, 68 days after launching.

Sixty-eight days after launching all that appears missing is the armament. There is a great deal of work going on inside: crews quarters, piping, wiring, navigation and engineering systems.

Courtesy National Maritime Museum.

back to San Francisco.' He wound up on a Liberty tanker (with a smaller engineroom)."

Finally, with the engine operating properly, the ship was put through the rest of her paces. At 0855 she passed through the submarine nets guarding the Golden Gate, clearing the bridge itself at 0859. Considering the fits and starts at the beginning, from this point on she did remarkably well. At first she was clocked at 17.0 knots, then at 17.5 knots. Finally, at 1300, near the Farallon Islands, she was run up to 105 r.p.m. and 9000 horsepower. Her speed was 18.0 knots! After a series of further maneuvering tests including a crash stop in which she was brought dead in the water in 1 minute and 15 seconds from full ahead, she was accepted. In time-honored tradition a broom was hoisted on her mainmast at 1445, showing a clean sweep of all tests. By 1953 that evening she was back at the dock ready for service.

As difficult as they were for engineers, the Mission tankers were an absolute pleasure for deck officers. Captain Anderson recalled, "They were just marvelous ships for maneuverability and handled beautifully."

Captain Anderson made the builders trials on the *Mission Santa Barbara* as chief mate.

"I was on there as she was delivered and as they were having trials. And the same way in Portland. I went out as chief mate on the *Corvallis*, which was a Swan Island T-2 and I was on trials there. It was amazing to take a look at that ship ten days before it was ready for delivery. You'd never expect it. And you'd see these people just swarming all over the place, Jeez there was one woman that would connect up all the yellow wires and another one would connect up the green ones and so on around the clock. It was just amazing. Everybody had a desire to do a job. And when it was delivered it was just like a brand new Cadillac off the assembly line."

When the *Mission Santa Ynez* was officially delivered on March 13, 1944 she joined seven of her sisters, previously turned over to the Maritime Commission. Twenty-six "Mission" style tankers would follow her for a total of 34 in the class. Their names and delivery dates were:

Mission Purisima	December 1943
Mission Santa Cruz	December 1943
Mission Soledad	January 1944
Mission San Jose	January 1944
Mission San Juan	January 1944
Mission San Miguel	February 1944

The pageantry and excitement of wartime launchings is captured in this photo of the launching of the Mission San Francisco.
Courtesy Bechtel Group, Inc.

Mission San Fernando	February 1944
Mission Santa Ynez	March 1944
Mission San Rafael	March 1944
Mission Solano	March 1944
Mission San Luis Rey	March 1944
Mission San Carlos	April 1944
Mission De Pala	April 1944
Mission San Diego	April 1944
Mission Carmel	May 1944
Mission San Antonio	May 1944
Mission San Gabriel	May 1944
Mission Dolores	May 1944
Mission Capistrano	June 1944
Mission Santa Clara	June 1944
Mission Buenaventura	June 1944
Mission Santa Barbara	July 1944
Mission San Luis Obispo	July 1944
Mission Loreto	July 1944
Mission Santa Maria	August 1944
Mission San Xavier	(completed as *Pasig AO-91*) August 1944
Mission San Lorenzo	(completed as *Abatan AO-92*) August 1944
Mission Santa Ana	(completed as *Soubarissen AO-93*) December 1944
Mission Alamo	(completed as *Anacostia AO-94*) January 1945
Mission Los Angeles	(completed as *Caney AO-95*) March 1945
Mission San Francisco	(completed as *Tamalpais AO-96*) April 1945
Concho AO-102	(completed as *Mission Santa Ana*) October 1945
Conecuh AO-103	(completed as *Mission Los Angeles*) October 1945
Contocook AO-104	(completed as *Mission San Francisco*)

The *Mission Santa Ynez* soon joined the war in the Pacific. What happened to her there would set the tone of her life for many years to come.

Shortly after outfitting, the Mission Santa Ynez, ready for sea.
Courtesy Marinship Museum.

November 10, 1943. The Mission Purisima *in San Francisco Bay on vessel trials. Looking at the forecastle gives one some sense of just how many people it took to put a vessel through her paces.*
San Francisco Maritime National Historical Park

November 23, 1943. The Mission Purisima on her sea trials, just prior to delivery to the Maritime Commission. Note the guns, rafts and lack of identification common to that era.

Credit: San Francisco Maritime National Historical Park

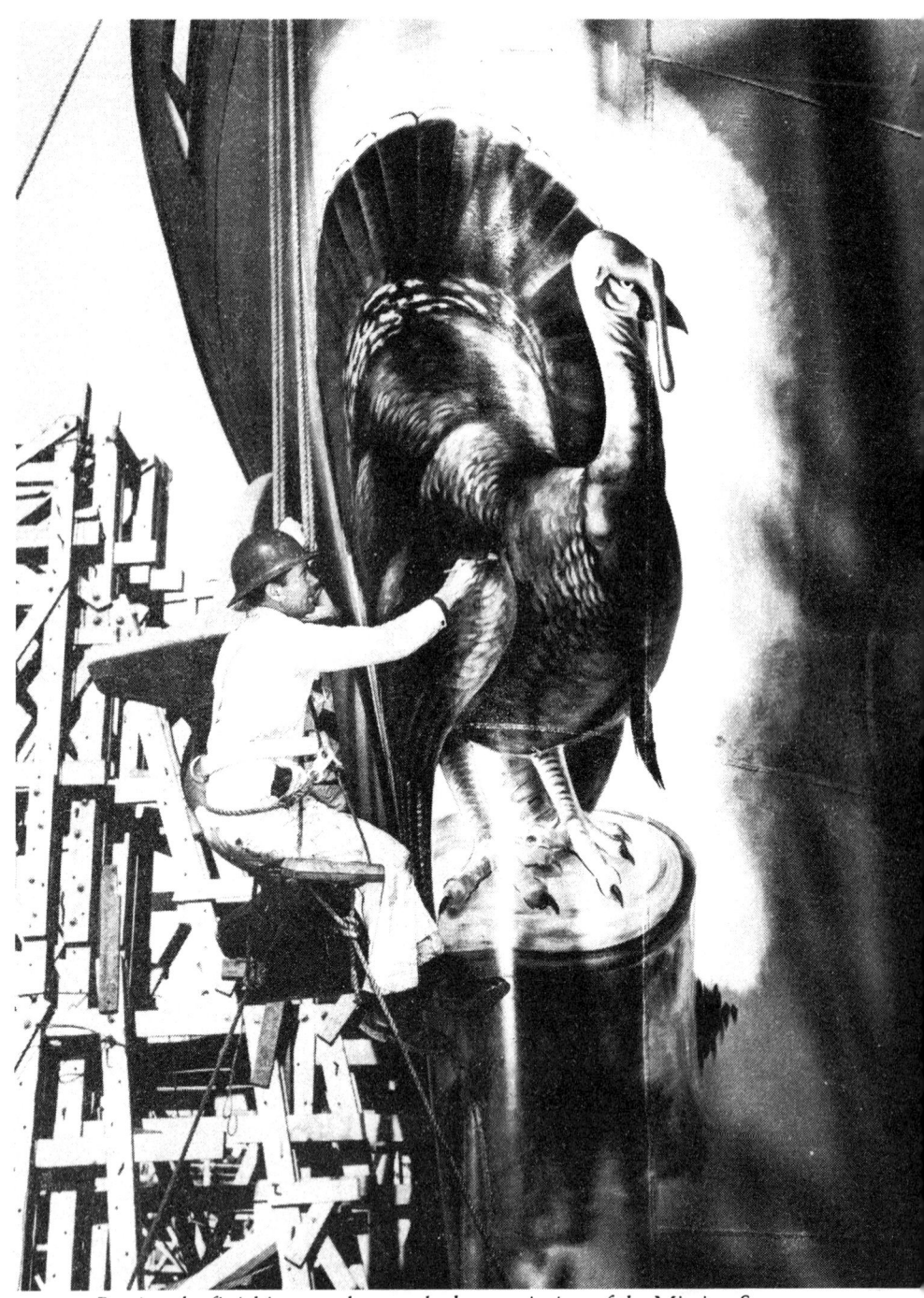

Putting the finishing touches on the bow painting of the Mission San Fernando. *This shot was taken in March of 1944. Perhaps the ship was launched around Thanksgiving time, hence the turkey.*
San Francisco Maritime National Historical Park

2 WAR MISSION

The *Mission Santa Ynez*' World War II record isn't found in the standard references. There is only the vague comment that she was "Chartered to Pacific Tankers, Inc. for operations, and spent the remainder of the war carrying fuel to our forces overseas." Captain Ted Anderson, however, remembered it well. As master of the ship on voyages four and five, he guided the vessel through much of its wartime career. As with everything else, the *Santa Ynez* worked through it, garnering no glory, but also without major disaster. There were bumps and grinds, dents and bruises. The realization grows that such things were her lot in life.

Captain Anderson's personal log lists key events as they occurred. His remembrances bring the war era to life.

September 25, 1944, joined ship at Balboa, Canal Zone. Relieved M.J. Ursin as master.

The first order of business after routine paper work was to make crew changes. The chief mate and one of the three radio operators (radio watches were 24 hours a day in wartime) were discharged. Two junior engineers were let go to allow them time to upgrade their licenses. Two crewmen were hospitalized and one deserted.

Captain Anderson was fortunate to have a chief engineer who was aware of the boiler problems in the Mission tankers.

"The first thing he did when he came on board that ship ... he figured, I'm going down in that engineroom ... and he pulled everyone of those handhold plugs, and God knows how many there were, off of there and took these gaskets off and then had his engineers sit there and cut the gaskets out of high pressure steam gasket material to put in place of those. We didn't have near the problems that most of these Mission ships had."

Like most merchant ships, the *Mission Santa Ynez* had her share of crew problems. One of Captain Anderson's first duties after joining the ship was to treat a gash in the electrician's head. Jack Saroyan was his name. He'd been hit with a two-inch dogging pipe by one of the departing crew. It took some effort, but the bleeding was stopped and he made the trip.

Because it was wartime, the crew problems were compounded. But there was also a spirit, a sense of pride, in making do. On one of his later voyages on a different ship in the Atlantic, Captain Anderson sailed with a chief mate he promoted on the basis of his having a Norwegian second mate's license. The two third mates, with no time on their licenses whatsoever, flipped a coin to see which would be the second mate. Fortunately on this voyage they sailed short only one crewman.

Sailed October 4, 1944 for high seas.

The cargo was aviation gasoline with a deck cargo of carrier-based Corsairs.

Wartime sailings were usually under sealed orders. Once the ship was safely at sea and the danger of a drunken crewman revealing the destination no longer existed, the orders were opened. Eniwetok was to be the first port of call.

Captain Anderson soon learned that chief engineer Maurice Doyle, was a highly skilled nuts-and-bolts operator, but somewhat lacking in technical skill.

"Doyle was a real great chief engineer. A real practical guy that could make things go. He didn't necessarily know the technical end of it. Whenever I'd go back there for lunch I'd stop in and say, 'well, have you got everything figured out?' And he'd be scratching around and, 'damn these figures don't come out.' And so I'd always ask him for a clean piece of paper and then I'd help him work his figures out.

"After a week or so he said, 'you know,' he says, 'I finally figured out what I'm doing wrong.' He said, 'I don't ever start out with a clean piece of paper.'"

October 24, 1944 arrived Eniwetok, Marshall Islands, 7200 miles out.

Tankers sailed individually to Eniwetok, but beyond that point went in convoy. After six or seven other ships arrived, a convoy conference was held at a quonset hut church ashore. The conference was to appoint a commander for the convoy, usually called the Convoy Commodore, and work out mutual understanding on position, signals, speed, destination and other details.

The conference of October 27th was to be special. Betty Hutton was on the island entertaining troops. The ships' officers were invited to see her performance after the conference. Unfortunately she canceled at the last minute, a victim of tropical food.

With the entertainment for the evening canceled, the only alternative was return to the ships. The port director provided his launch to ferry the officers back to their vessels. Ted Anderson describes what happened next:

"This one skipper from the east coast invited us all on his ship for a couple of drinks. It was a hell of a messy ship, rust all over creation. He was one of these skippers that insisted that the chief steward prepare the *hors d'oeuvres*, and have a towel over his arm and he'd serve the *hors d'oeuvres*. We're up there in his quarters having a few drinks and having these *hors d'oeuvres*, and supposed to sail the next day. So he launched his motor life boat to take us back to our ship. We get down into this motor life boat and the skipper decides that he's going to be the helmsman and he's got the chief engineer down cranking on this god damn engine and he couldn't get the thing started. He hadn't had the clutch in. We finally took off and the skipper went ass over teakettle and we bailed him out of the water."

October 28, 1944 Depart for Ulithi, Western Caroline Islands.

One of the more colorful officers was the Chief Mate, Gustof Thoren. Born in Sweden, he was a naturalized citizen with a master's license for sailing vessels; a rare accomplishment. Captain Anderson remembered him as: "... a fine old gentleman and a real good chief mate. He didn't like people that smoked cigarettes. I used to smoke cigarettes, so did the rest of the officers. I got everyone to agree that when Thoren came in to eat his meals we wouldn't smoke. You know what he'd do? He'd have a box of cigars and then he'd smoke his cigars in his room and after they got really saturated with nicotine about that long (holding up thumb and forefinger about one inch apart) he'd take a pocket knife and he'd cut these pieces up and put'em in one of these safety match boxes. Then he'd chew those damn things while he was on watch."

The most dangerous passage for the *Mission Santa Ynez* during this time was from Eniwetok to Ulithi. The Island of Truk was bypassed in earlier battles and still occupied by the Japanese. The course past it to Ulithi was close enough to make everyone more concerned than usual. The fear was that they might be shelled from the island or attract enemy airplanes. Submarines, however, were not a problem. As Ted Anderson said, "The Japanese just didn't have it put together when it came to submarine warfare.

Arrived Ulithi November 1, 1944. Discharged cargo, took on 50 tons fresh water.

There was some excitement after the anchors were dropped in Ulithi. A miniature Japanese submarine was spotted inside the atoll. Navy destroyers went into action crisscrossing the area with depth charges. Whether the sub was sunk is unknown. It was not seen again.

November 3, sailed for Balboa.

Because of the ever-present threat of enemy attack, ships traveled blacked out at night. This caused problems with collisions and near misses. Adding to the difficulty was the fact that only the Navy had radar. One such near-miss occurred on the *Santa Ynez*, however, during the day time. "... headed for Panama. You run into these damn rain squalls in the South Pacific. It was obviously a Navy ship and I'm not sure what kind of a Navy ship 'cause I couldn't even see him until he was practically on top of us. We were going along and off the starboard bow we get this challenge by blinker. And so I wonder really which way this guy is heading. Obviously 'cause I couldn't see him, he must have had radar. He had to be a Navy ship. I just held our course and speed. Pretty soon there he was just off the starboard bow! God, I hauled over hard right and when I passed that guy I could smell and feel the heat right out of his stack as soon as he went by. I went out on the left wing of the bridge and I screamed at that bastard, called him every name I could think of. Oh, God. Talk, about a thrill."

The armament was handled by a navy gun crew. According to Ted Anderson, the reason the merchant crew didn't handle the guns was, "If they were caught handling guns in case of war, you'd get shot for piracy. But if you were in the military, then you were held as a prisoner of war,"

Most gun crews had little or no experience at sea. Some were good and some not. The *Santa Ynez*'s was not. It seemed to hinge on the officer in charge.

"This guy had never been to sea. He was in a little small newspaper in the midwest. He was a Lieutenant j.g. in charge of the gun crew. As far as he was concerned everybody on the ship was his buddy. He'd wander around in his shorts and fraternize

Part of a vessel's acceptance trials includes testing the steering engine. The Mission Purisima making a hard right turn on November 10, 1943. Note the framing above the main deck. Tankers commonly carried airplanes as cargo on such framework during World War II. San Francisco Maritime National Historical Park

with everybody as though he was interviewing them for a newspaper. So the discipline went to hell in the gun crew. So I raised hell with him a couple of times and when we finally got to San Pedro I went to the port director and told him that this guy had to be removed. He was no damn good and he didn't maintain any discipline and he didn't have any regular routines with his men and they got sloppy and caused problems with the rest of the crew so they promptly removed him. Later I had a full Lieutenant and he was a real able fellow."

November 24, 1944 arrived in Balboa for minor repairs. Discharged 2nd mate Michael J. O'Conner. Was able to hospitalize. Signed off pumpman and one A.B. with sick relatives, mutual consent.

Michael J. O'Conner had gone to sea during the first World War. Since then he farmed in the midwest somewhere, but kept his second mate's license up to date. At the age of seventy he came back to do his part for the War effort. Unfortunately time had passed him by. He had no comprehension of what was going on. Captain Anderson was relieved to be rid of him.

In peacetime seamen sign articles for the duration of the voyage, that is from first United States port of loading until return to that port. Anyone who tried to leave the vessel earlier was disciplined. The stress of war eased many such rules. A crewman could sign off a ship during wartime if he had sick relatives. But he had to document such a hardship. If able to do so, he asked to be discharged and normally the master agreed. Such a departure is commonly referred to as discharge by "mutual consent."

December 3, 1944 sailed Balboa after having exceedingly difficult time storing ship properly.

The union representative on this voyage wasn't too popular with the crew. His full beard seemed to be a badge of office and became a focal point of the crew's dislike. While painting the ship they managed to "spill" enough paint in the beard to make him shave it off.

During wartime many regulations were relaxed, including those that pertained to animals on board ship. The *Mission Santa Ynez*'s mascot during this time was a black and grey alley cat.

"I think the poor bugger got his tail caught in the steering engine or something. Because it had a bend in it like that (drawing two opposing right angles in the air). And this guy, Thoren, being an old Swede ... we'd be sailing along deep in the water and the fly-

The Mission Purisima on vessel trials, 1943. Bristling with guns, like all the Mission tankers, she appears ready for action.
San Francisco Maritime National Historical Park

ing fish would wind up on deck. And Thoren, he'd make the rounds out there to pick up the flying fish and he'd have the steward fix'em up for breakfast. So it was a race between this damn cat and Thoren to see who'd get the flying fish first. You'd see that cat walking up the deck. You'd see old Thoren out there, scowling at the cat."

December 23, 1944 arrived Eniwetok, Marshall Islands.

December 25, alongside Plattsburg to top off. Jacinski bos'n on her.

Seafaring people have a knack of running in to each other in the most unexpected places. Sometimes the run in is both literal and figurative. On Christmas day the *Plattsburg* and the *Mission Santa Ynez* went alongside each other to transfer fuel. In the process they came together rather sharply causing some damage to the *Ynez*'s after boat deck. Once the excitement had passed and the ships were tied together, Captain Anderson looked over to the other ship and saw a familiar face. There was Jacinski, a friend from his Standard Oil days in Alaska. The boatswain was from the Russian fishing village of Ninotchik in Alaska, one of Anderson's old haunts. Jacinski later became master of one of the Alaska Ferries.

December 27, 1944 Depart in company with Dan Thompson (Great White Father) Mission San Antonio."

So then we had this convoy conference. There was this chap that was the commodore skipper for the Standard of California fleet, by the name of Dan Thompson. Everybody called him the Great White Father. He retired and he went skipper on the *San Antone*. So we ran in to him in Eniwetok. This port director would send this boat to pick us up to go to the convoy conference. Dan was in the boat. Of course I knew him. He didn't know too much about me. He knew that I'd been with Standard Oil. So in this very haughty, sneering way he said 'this war has done marvels for you young people' and so forth. Just snotty as hell.

"It was interesting because this was on the second trip out there for me. There were two entrances to this atoll. One was on the east side and one was on the south. When we were leaving on this convoy we were supposed to go out through the southern entrance to this atoll. And old Dan, he would be damned if he would go that way. He would go out the way he came in. Then he really had to hook it up to come around to get back into the convoy. So

DEPARTMENT OF TRANSPORTATION

UNITED STATES COAST GUARD

FORECASTLE CARD

CG 704
(Rev. 3-67)

Notice is hereby given that section 4519 of the U. S. Revised Statutes (U. S. C., title 46, sec. 577) makes it obligatory on the part of the master of a merchant vessel of the United States, at the commencement of every voyage or engagement, to cause a legible copy of the agreement (omitting signatures) to be placed or posted up in such part of the vessel as to be accessible to the crew, under a penalty not exceeding ONE HUNDRED DOLLARS.

ARTICLES OF AGREEMENT BETWEEN MASTER AND SEAMEN IN THE MERCHANT SERVICE OF THE UNITED STATES

Required by act of Congress, title LIII, Revised Statutes of the United States (U. S. C., title 46, chap. 18)

Office of the U. S. Shipping Commissioner for the Port of Manchester, Wash. 12/19, 1973.

IT IS AGREED between the master and seamen, or mariners, of the USNS MISSION SANTA YNEZ
of which Calvin W. Henderson

is at present master, or whoever shall go for master, now bound from the port of (1) Manchester, Washington , to on a tramp tanker voyage, either direct or via one or more Coastwise ports, to ports on the U.S. Pacific, Atlantic, Gulf or Great Lakes Coast and/or to ports in the Caribbean Sea and/or European ports and/or African ports and/or ports in the Near or Far East and/or Australia

GOING ON SHORE IN FOREIGN PORTS IS PROHIBITED EXCEPT BY PERMISSION OF THE MASTER

NO DANGEROUS WEAPONS (1) OR GROG ALLOWED, AND NONE TO BE BROUGHT ON BOARD BY THE CREW

SCALE OF PROVISIONS to be allowed and served out to the crew during the voyage in addition to the daily issue of lime juice and lemon juice and sugar, or other antiscorbutics in any case required by law

		Sunday	Monday	Tuesday	Wednesday	Thursday	Friday	Saturday			Sunday	Monday	Tuesday	Wednesday	Thursday	Friday	Saturday
Water	quarts	½	6	6	6	6	6	5	Coffee (green berry)	ounces	¾	¾	¾	¾	¾	¾	¾
Biscuit	pounds	½	¾	½	¾	½	½	½	Tea	ounces	3	3	3	3	3	3	3
Beef, salt	pounds		1	1¼	1	1¼	1	1¼	Sugar	ounces	3	3	3	3	3	3	3
Pork, salt	pounds								Molasses	pint							
Flour	pound	¼		½	½	½	½	½	Dried fruit	ounces							
Canned meat	pound								Pickles	pint	½	½	½	½	½	½	½
Fresh bread	pounds	1½		1½	1½	1½	1½	1½	Vinegar	pint							
Fish, dry, preserved, or fresh	pound								Corn meal	ounces							
Potatoes or yams	pound	1	1	1	1	1	1	1	Onions	ounces	4				4		
Canned tomatoes	pound	½					½	½	Lard	ounce	2	2	2	2	2	2	2
Peas	pint								Butter	ounce							
Beans	pint	½	¼	½	¼				Mustard, pepper, and salt sufficient for seasoning								
Rice	pint																

The Forecastle Card lists the minimum provisions allowed the crew as well as serving notice to them of some of the dos and don'ts of the voyage.

he had too much speed going when we were just forming up out there. You could see him out the wing of the bridge waving his arms around like crazy, backing full astern, slowing down, disrupting the whole convoy."

December 31, 1944 arrived in Ulithi.

"When we got to Ulithi, we went ashore to see the port director. Dan was in the boat. I made the comment, 'you know, Dan,' I said. 'It's always safe to go out the way you came in, but Jesus you sure as hell screwed up the convoy.'

"Jesus, he was just furious."

Apparently the Great White Father wasn't one to hold a grudge. The following entry shows they continued on a friendly basis.

January 5, 1945 M.M. Doyle and self visited great white father.

During the stay in Ulithi a typhoon hit the atoll. Receiving short notice, Captain Anderson made sure both anchors were well placed. Then he pumped water into the available empty tanks to bring the ship down in the water and present less hull surface to the winds. When the storm hit the engines had to be operated at various speeds according to wind velocity, just to keep the ship from dragging.

During the same stay, when time allowed, they hoisted anchor, shifted to a different location in the atoll, and sent the crew ashore in a lifeboat for a swimming party.

With such a long stay in port there were social occasions. Periodically the officers from one ship had dinner on another. Sometimes things got out of hand, especially if the subject were politics.

"I invited the captain and chief engineer over for a couple of drinks and to have dinner with us. Doyle was there and he was a very staunch Republican, hated the Roosevelts. He didn't like Mrs. Roosevelt almost as much as he didn't like President Roosevelt. The chief engineer off the other ship was named McPherson. So after dinner we went up and had one more nightcap. Then we got into this political argument about the Roosevelts. The other Captain and myself kind of stayed out of it because we were kind of getting a big kick out of it. McPherson was a rather pompous individual. He kept needling my chief engineer about what fine people the Roosevelts were. Doyle just absolutely ranted and raved. We were drinking Ballantine's Scotch and I've never had another drink of

With a bone in her teeth, the Mission Purisima *underway on San Francisco Bay during her vessel trials in 1943. Viewed head on, a Mission tanker was a formidable ship.*

San Francisco Maritime National Historical Park

Ballantine's Scotch since, 'cause the next day, Jesus, I felt like hell. But Doyle finally concluded the argument by telling McPherson that Mrs. Roosevelt wouldn't make a good centerpiece for a bouquet of backsides. McPherson decided that was enough. They took off and went back to their ship."

January 24, 1945. Depart after long awaited discharge of 24 days. Short on food and water. Rationed food for past two weeks and water for past month. Discharged into 12 ships.

January 29, 1945 D.W., Wiper seriously ill. Unable to stand without passing out. Confined to hospital for treatment.

Long periods of time at sea without the sight of a woman tend to make seamen passionate when they finally do get ashore. The result of this passion is frequently some form of social disease. In the era before penicillin such diseases could be debilitating. Sulfa drugs were the prescribed cure during World War II.

"He wound up with the crud, so I started treating him with sulfa drugs and he violently reacted. Jesus he couldn't take it. So we got no work out of him for the whole voyage ... and got back to Panama and got rid of him. A few months later I go back to New York. We start out in the convoy and the first thing you do of course is have fire and boat drill to make sure everybody is going to be on deck and know what the hell they're supposed to do. So this one guy didn't show up for fire and boat drill. Didn't pay any attention to the name. So I asked the chief engineer, I says, 'bring this fellow up. Let me have a talk with him. He comes up and it's the same damn guy I didn't get any work out of him on the *Santa Ynez*. So I told the chief, I said, 'that guy was on the *Santa Ynez*. We didn't get one day's work out of him. Now you put him to work, no overtime, no nothing. Just work his butt off.' That guy was the first one off when we got back to New York."

February 9, 1945. 12 noon. Unable to proceed on to Balboa do to water shortage have diverted to San Pedro.

Despite Chief Doyle's best efforts, the temperature/pressure/gasket problems inherent to the Mission tankers caught up with the *Mission Santa Ynez*. Valuable fresh water was lost operating the boilers and the ship had to put into San Pedro rather than make her intended destination of Balboa.

"You don't like to not carry out your voyage. That chief felt real bad, but you had to make up your mind. And we couldn't

Stern view of the Mission Purisima *on sea trials in 1943. The cleanliness of the steel, from stack to rudder post, shows how new she is.*
San Francisco Maritime National Historical Park

make enough water. We were beating on those coils on that evaporator regularly. It was just miserable."

While Captain Anderson didn't condone drinking, he could be tolerant if it was kept in bounds. Some lessons he learned the hard way. The union representative came to him with the request that he be given a bottle to share with the rest of the crew to celebrate his birthday the following day. The captain agreed and that night the union representative and his watch partner were drunk and no one else got a taste. It was the last time Ted Anderson ever did that.

February 13, 1945 arrived San Pedro quarantine anchorage.

February 14, 1945 fast alongside Standard Shipbuilding Corp. San Pedro.

March 1, 1945 relieved for vacation by Captain Eastman.

Captain Anderson always had a warm spot in his heart for the *Mission Santa Ynez*. Although not literally his first ship, he felt like it was his first as captain.

"The other one just didn't leave any impression because it was a very short voyage to the Caribbean and back. But with this ship ... I'll tell you when I was sailing in the fo'c'sle, I thought if I ever got to be a third mate that I'd have it made for life. When you got to be third mate, normally you had a master's license. In fact, when I went to work for Standard Oil, there were a lot of masters in the fo'c'sle. So you can imagine how I must have felt when I got to be master of the *Mission Santa Ynez*. I mean it was just like it was my own personal domain and personal ship. I don't think I was egotistical about it. But I look back on it and I think to myself, I hadn't yet turned 24, and I thought, my gosh, here I started out on a lousy cannery tender running around Cook's Inlet picking up fish and wasn't even a skipper but a deck hand. And then I wind up as skipper on a brand new great big ship that sailed all around the world. Of all the ships that I sailed on, this by far has more of a feel to me ... That *Santa Ynez* was a great ship."

Months passed for the *Mission Santa Ynez* on the same route — Balboa, Eniwetok, Ulithi, Balboa — with an occasional side trip through the canal to Aruba. Finally with the arrival of VJ day, she was no longer needed. Unheralded and unsung, she was returned to the Maritime Commission and placed in the James River Reserve Fleet at Fort Eustace, Virginia in 1946. It was to be a short rest.

3
MISSIONS OF PEACE

Her lay-up was short-lived for on October 22, 1947 the *Mission Santa Ynez* was acquired by the Navy and designated *AO-134*. In October of 1949, the newly formed Military Sea Transport Service (MSTS) took her over and officially renamed her *USNS Mission Santa Ynez (T-AO-134)*. On the same date, October 1, she was chartered to Mathiasen's Tanker Industries, Inc. It was a relationship which was to last many years.

Again she served the nation faithfully without recognition or record. We find no trace of her until 1955. Meanwhile attrition was taking its toll on her sisters.

In 1955 the *Soubarissen AO-94* (laid down as the *Mission Santa Ana*) was laid up in the Beaumont Reserve Fleet, near Port Arthur, Texas. She was the first of the *Ynez*'s sisters to leave postwar service.

At some point the *Mission Santa Ynez* and *Soubarissen* crossed paths for the *Ynez* was in Port Arthur on January 1 of that year. From there she went to Houston and Savannah.

Certain lives seem fated to ever struggle against vicissitude. For such, there comes a time when the person — or the ship — reaches a turning point — to finally succumb and fall under the wheels of fate or to develop a determined invincibility, an undaunted refusal to capitulate to the seeming will of the gods. This quiet, anonymous triumph over adversity, the ultimate test of the strength of spirit and will, was one characteristic of the *Mission Santa Ynez*.

We pick up her story in Skagway, Alaska on April 14, 1955. While attempting to dock starboard side to, the *Mission Santa Ynez* was blown into the dock by a strong SSW wind. The overhang on the bow in the area of the anchor windlass collided with the pier, causing three pilings to splinter and fifteen feet of the forecastle gunwale to be bent inward. Because of the wind and tide, the captain had to turn the ship around, drop the starboard anchor, and moor port side to the pier.

On July 3, 1955 we find the ship in Sondrestrom, Greenland, under command of a different master. The ship was tied off to three mooring buoys with the port anchor out, discharging cargo into a submarine pipeline that came to the surface close to the starboard side. She was pointing due west. Came sailing time and the wind blew strongly out of the east. The lines tied to the mooring buoys astern were normally released by having a soldier stand on the buoy and cut them with an axe. Just as the Captain gave the order to let go, the soldier fell off the buoy, dropping his axe. This left the wind blowing the stern of the vessel into the pipeline apparatus. Rather than allow that to happen, the captain ordered the third mate on the stern to simply let the lines go into the water. He was then able to maneuver the ship away from the pipeline and buoys without causing any damage. One of the assisting tugs immediately picked the soldier up out of the frigid waters of the arctic circle. A near disaster with loss of life was averted.

That same month, in the port of Narssuak, Greenland, there was another incident. On July 27, the ship was forced to lay off the entrance to the port due to "... congested ice conditions, strong SE winds, and low visibility ..." At 1700 the bow collided with a small growler (iceberg). The result was a 2½ inch dent in the hull. Fortunately, there were no leaks.

The *Ynez'* series of minor but aggravating incidents continued in Jacksonville, Florida on September 22 the same year. She was tied to the USN Fuel Depot, Trout River, Jacksonville. After discharging aviation gasoline, the local pilot began backing the vessel away from the dock. Being starboard side to the dock, one tug pushed on the port bow while the other pulled on the port quarter. The forepart of the ship struck a concrete and steel piling that was part of the dock. The result was another dent in the hull plating near the #2 starboard cargo tank.

It was in March of 1957 that the first of the Mission tankers was lost. Sailing in the Delaware River, in ballast but not gas-free, the *Mission San Francisco* collided with the *Elna II*. The tanker's mid-body disintegrated in the ensuing explosion, leaving the bow and stern intact and the river bottom littered with small pieces of tangled wreckage. The aft section of the ship was refloated in May. But while being towed to Philadelphia there was another collision, this time with a Liberian-flag oil/ore carrier, the *Cosmic*. The sad

MEET THE MSTS FLEET—(18) USNS MISSION SANTA YNEZ

This month's "back cover ship," the *Mission Santa Ynez*, takes on jet fuel at Houston. See page 23 for details about her and her sister tankers.

—SERVICE TO THE SERVICES—

U.S. Army • U.S. Air Force • U.S. Navy • U.S. Marine Corps

MILITARY SEA TRANSPORTATION SERVICE

SEALIFT MAGAZINE • SEPTEMBER 1963

The Mission Santa Ynez *taking on fuel in Houston in 1963.*
Courtesy Department of the Navy.

remains of the *Mission San Francisco* arrived at the Philadelphia Navy base on June 1 and were finally scrapped in Boston the following year.

On May 28, 1957, at about the same time the *San Francisco*'s stern was raised, we find the *Mission Santa Ynez*, ever the workhorse, in Whittier, Alaska serving under yet another master. With a full cargo she was attempting to get alongside the POL pier with the assistance of an Army tug, the *LT-648* pushing on the stern. In the process of doing so, the tug pushed against the after welldeck railing, breaking 4 stanchions, three pieces of pipe rail, and bending approximately 20 feet of additional pipe rail.

The gallant ship struggled on. During the same voyage, a few days later, she touched bottom coming into Kodiak. There was no damage.

The second Mission tanker to be lost was the *Mission San Miguel*. On October 9, 1957 on a voyage from Guam to Seattle, the ship ran aground on Laysan Reef, 775 miles NW of Hawaii. At the time, Captain Anderson was General Superintendent of Pacific Tankers. He remembered the incident well. "... there was a skipper on her ... we were operating her for MSTS ... by the name of Countryman. And Countryman was probably the oldest timer and one of the best seafaring men on the Pacific Coast as far as tankers were concerned; an excellent seaman, excellent navigator and everything else. And I'll be damned if out in some place between the Caroline Islands or the Marshall Islands and Honolulu he winds up hitting a reef. Uncharted reef. And that ship was lost out there.

"I happened to be in New York at the time and got word of this and immediately went from New York to Washington, D.C., 'cause that Admiral Wills was the head honcho (for MSTS). So I figured, 'I'll go and listen to him blast off about losing this ship.' And so I went in and, Jesus, that guy ranted and raved for at least forty-five minutes. He was gonna hang the captain by his thumbs.

"Nobody was lost. They were all picked up. And the reef was totally uncharted."

The *Mission San Miguel* was declared a constructive total loss, abandoned, and stricken from the government registers. In later years it was used as a bombing target.

In 1958 the *Mission Purisima* and the *Mission Santa Ana* were laid up in the Suisun Bay Reserve Fleet near San Francisco, California.

In 1959 two additional Mission tankers were laid up, the *Mission Los Angeles* on August 13, 1959 at the James River

The Mission Dolores alongside a San Francisco pier in 1948. Note absence of gun tubs and use of wording "U.S. Naval Tanker" rather than "U.S. Naval Ship" which was used when M.S.T.S. took over the vessel. San Francisco Maritime National Historical Park

Reserve Fleet near Norfolk, Virginia and the *Mission Loreto* at Suisun Bay.

Meanwhile we find the *Mission Santa Ynez* in St. Johns, Newfoundland on August 2nd, 1959. From there she retraced her steps to San Pedro, California. Thence to Yokohama and the Suez, which she transited on February 25, 1960.

While many of her sisters were idle, the *Ynez* was hard at work. Several months were spent in support work for the Sixth Fleet in the Mediterranean. During this period she conducted 32 underway replenishment at sea operations with the *USS Waccamaw (AO-109)*, *USS Chukawan (AO-100)*, *USS Missinewa (AO-144)* and USN Mine Division #85. She also suffered the most serious collision in her history.

According to the official report she was instructed to rendezvous with and transfer fuel to the *USS Waccamaw (AO-109)* on October 13, 1960. Following instructions from the Navy ship, the *Santa Ynez* steered a course of 125 degrees true, at a speed of 12 knots. She was in position at 0911 with the *Waccamaw* taking her position alongside to starboard at 1006. The sea was moderate and the swell heavy from astern. By 1026 lines and hoses were in place and discharging began. At 1135 the master of the *Ynez* noticed the other vessel was having difficulty maneuvering and shut down the cargo pumps. At 1136 the *Mission Santa Ynez* was ordered to stand by for emergency breakaway. At 1137 the master of the *Ynez* received orders to swing to port, which he did immediately while at the same time breaking away the hoses and lines. At 1140 both vessels were on parallel courses, steadied up, touched together momentarily, and parted on a heading of 170 degrees true. By 1142 all refueling gear was clear.

The combined effects of tens of thousands of tons of steel ship and cargo "touching together momentarily" at twelve knots is formidable. 154 feet of hull plating was pushed in, from two inches in some places to ten inches in others.

One of the more humiliating consequences of damage to a ship is that everyone has to get a copy of the incident report. In addition to the steamship company, reports go to the company's nearest agent, the Commander-in-Chief of MSTS, the Navy, the Judge Advocate General's office in Washington, D.C., the company's legal office, the insurance underwriters, and the nearest Coast Guard Office. The whole world, it seems, knows about the embarrassing mishap. It can't just be forgotten after the repairs are made, or drowned in a bottle of scotch.

The Mission Santa Ana with steam up, awaiting a cargo alongside a San Francisco pier. Probably taken around 1949 as there are no gun tubs on the ship. Note "Acme Beer" sign on building on right. The vessel on the right looks like a C-4. San Francisco Maritime National Historical Park

Then it almost happened again. Just a few weeks later the ship was fueling the *USS Chukawan* (*AO-100*). After connecting lines and hoses, the *Ynez* began pumping at 1035 on the morning of November 4, 1960. At 1114 the pumps were stopped. The *Chukawan* was out of control with a steering gear failure. Fortunately there was no damage. The *Ynez*'s time required for emergency breakaway had improved a great deal.

Having large areas of their midbody devoid of framework, tankers lend themselves to the economies of being cut up and made into other types of ships. This lack of internal framework requires added strength, in the initial construction, in the longitudinal supports to give the hull its needed rigidity. This in turn makes the ship naturally strong; an added plus in a conversion. In 1961 the first of many conversions on a Mission tanker took place. The *Mission Capistrano* was made into a sound testing experimental ship. Installing a five story high transducer assembly, Todd Shipyards Corp. of New Orleans fitted the vessel to detect submarines at long distances. Located just aft of the bridge, the massive transducer could be raised and lowered at will. The ship was also fitted with experimental station keeping devices. Two 1250 horsepower electric motors were fitted with 7-foot four-bladed propellers which could be rotated 360 degrees. These were driven by computers which in turn were fed by either Loran-C signals or hydrophone bearings working off an acoustic beacon on the ocean floor. In a typical test, as part of project Artemis taking place off Texas Tower Argus Island near Bermuda, the ship performed remarkably. While in 13,000 feet of water her average deviation from position was 142 feet and the maximum 241 feet, with the winds blowing 28 knots and gusting to 35 in a 5 foot sea and 11 foot swell.

After a brief period in layup in the James River Fleet, the vessel was converted to a drilling ship and renamed *Capistrano*.

Tankers are efficient ships. They load and discharge cargo quickly, often staying in port for only a few hours. With limited shore leave, it takes stable men to put up with the rigors of tanker duty. "Tankeritis" is the term often used among seamen to refer to the effects of smelling petroleum fumes for extended periods and spending too much time at sea. The *Mission Santa Ynez* had her share of such people.

Unfortunately there are fumes other than petroleum to contend with ashore. One of the able-bodied seamen assigned as quartermaster on the 12 to 4 watch received four warnings before he was finally logged. On November 1, 1960 he failed to turn to when the vessel unmoored at Augusta, Sicily. The following day he

The Mission Dolores, almost full and down, alongside a San Francisco Bay pier some time between 1947 and 1950.
San Francisco Maritime National Historical Park

missed the entire day's work and again on November 3rd. On May 18 he missed his watch. He was again logged on May 24, 1961 in Subic Bay, Philippine Islands for again not standing his watch. In addition, with the sailing board set for 1400 he just staggered aboard as the ship was leaving and couldn't turn to because of "being under the influence of alcohol."

The second cook and baker was logged on February 4, 1961, at sea for being "unable to perform his duty due to being under the influence of alcoholic beverage: searching his quarters, master confiscated and destroyed 1½ quart bottles of whisky."

Another able-bodied seaman was logged in Sasebo, Japan, on March 10 and 11, 1961, "Due to intoxication, unable to finish standing his assigned watch from 2000 to 2400 on 3/10/61; unable to turn to 0800 to 1200 and was not on board 2000 to 2400 to stand his watch on 3/11/61; unable to shift ship from 1600 to 1700 on 3/11/61."

Sasebo was an epidemic to the crew and the ship. From the log: "... Due to intoxication, unable to finish standing his assigned 2000 to 2400 watch on 3/10/61. On 3/11/61 ... At 1600 to 1700, did not turn to to shift ship ... Was not on board to stand his assigned 2000 to 2400 watch on 3/11/61. On 3/11/61 at 0900 he told Master that he was not afraid of the Master and would take him out on the dock emphasizing same by what the Master could do ..."

The 2nd pumpman was logged, "After having carry over of both boilers, was relieved, unable to stand watch apparently under the influence of liquor."

One of the worst was another able-bodied Seaman who was drunk for a solid week. "At ports Derince and Augusta and at sea, ... was unable to perform his duties due to being under the influence of liquor. On 30 June 1961, Master, Chief Mate & Chief Engineer searched vessel for contraband. Found four (4) full bottles (two of which were quart bottles) PLUS 3 partially filled bottles all with liquor belonging to _____."

This same character was logged along with everyone else in Sasebo on March 11 for being too drunk to work.

But fate or luck is cyclical; there are ups as well as downs. After her misadventures in the Mediterranean and the Far East, the *Mission Santa Ynez* got a chance to redeem her reputation.

It started with the radio operator intercepting a message to the Coast Guard in Miami. "NOTE TO US CG MIAMI X ERE M/V SOLENGEN/DIKX GERMAN X DRIFTING OPEN BOAT, 306 DEGREES ALLIGATOR 17 MLS LAT 2436

The radio room of the Mission Santa Ynez. *It was here the message was received about the Cuban refugees.*
Credit the author

NORTH LONG 8030 WEST X 9 (NINE) PEOPLE IN DISTRESS. PLEASES HELP AT ONCE X ERE STANDING BY GERMAN M/V SOLENGEN/DIKX"

The captain calculated the *Mission Santa Ynez*'s position as being 3 hours' run from the distress position. He advised the Coast Guard and offered assistance.

The Coast Guard asked the tanker to proceed to the location and assist the refugees.

Arriving shortly before midnight on October 28, 1961, the *Mission Santa Ynez* hove to and awaited developments. The German ship was drifting with a small boat tied off her stern. In the boat were the nine Cuban refugees: six men and three women ranging in age from 20 to 35. Reluctant to take them on board for the trip to Europe, the German ship was waiting for a ship inbound for Florida, that could put the refugees ashore quickly.

Because of the weather it took three and a half hours to get them aboard. One of the crewmen risked his life in the process and received a letter of commendation from Mathiasen's Tanker Industries, Inc.

"It has been brought to my attention by Captain E. Monaghan, master to the *Mission Santa Ynez* that you risked your life to save the life of a Cuban refugee. Every one here joins me in commending you for this outstanding action ... we would like to have your permission to recommend you for the Annual United Seaman's Service Life Saving Award.

Yours Very Truly,
J.A. Engelbrecht
Vice President, Operations"

Due to the presence of the refugees, the ship had to go into quarantine at Tampa, rather than proceeding directly to her scheduled drydocking.

The up-cycle didn't last long. A little over a year later we find the long-suffering ship in Kingston, Jamaica, alongside the *USS Yosemite* transferring fresh water to that ship. Captain Moretti, her master for many years, explained what happened in his letter to Mathiasen's.

"At 1206, the *Mission Santa Ynez* was ready to leave, it was planned to let the stern, breast and spring lines go, and heave on the bow line to separate the stern of both ships away from each other, then back the *Mission Santa Ynez* away.

"When the stern of both vessels was the maximum distance from each other, the bow line was let go. At 1218, Half Speed

The Mission Purisima alongside a San Francisco pier in 1946. The hull coloring shows she has carried many loads and is due for drydocking.
San Francisco Maritime National Historical Park

Astern on the *Mission Santa Ynez*, with hard left rudder. Everything proceeded according to plan, except the wind which from calm, commenced blowing from the SE, force about 2, and blew the stern of the *USS Yosemite* down on the *Mission Santa Ynez*. At 1220, both vessels came together. There was some crunching, which started at the after end of the midship house, and ended when this part of the vessel was clear, at about 1221.

"During the short interval the two vessels were rubbing together — Full Astern and Full ahead was tried — to minimize the damage. These engine maneuvers did not provide the desired result ...

"The damage to the *USS Yosemite* consisted of about (40) feet of three (3) tier hand railing and four (4) stanchions, supporting these railings, which were repaired by *USS Yosemite* ship force.

"The sea worthiness of the *USNS Mission Santa Ynez* was not impaired.

"The master was doing the piloting.

"Repair requisition covering this damage will be submitted."

In January of 1963 the *Mission Santa Clara* was transferred to the Pakistan Navy under the Mutual Defense Aid Program and renamed *Dacca*.

Four months later the *Santa Ynez* was at Charleston, South Carolina. But it seemed her fate to deal with ineptitude. Arriving off the sea buoy on the morning of April 22, 1963, a pilot was taken aboard and the vessel proceeded toward the US Army Transportation Dock at North Charleston. At 0832 while rounding Meyers Bend, marked by buoy #48, a tug and barge were seen coming in the opposite direction, downstream. The *Ynez*'s pilot sounded a short blast on the whistle meaning he wanted to pass port to port. This was answered by two blasts from the tug (meaning he wanted to pass starboard to starboard) which then unaccountably changed course to port — in the direction of the ship. The pilot immediately stopped the engine and blew the danger signal, followed by a single blast. The tug once more answered with two blasts. The pilot again blew the danger signal. The tug and barge didn't answer and held their course. At 0833 the bow of the barge hit the port side of the *Mission Santa Ynez* between tanks five and six, and scraped its way along the side of the ship.

When the *Mission Santa Ynez* finally got alongside the dock and the captain rang down Finished With Engines, it was with the knowledge that he was in for yet another round of questions and

The Mission Santa Ana under commercial livery. Note the stack marking. At a San Francisco pier, probably around 1950. Is that Treasure Island in the background on the left? San Francisco Maritime National Historical Park

answers, letters and reports, with copies going to what seemed like half the civilized world.

Meanwhile other Mission ships were selected to a more noble calling. With the target date of having a man on the moon by 1970, the Apollo Project required long range planning. In September of 1964 the *Mission San Juan, Mission De Pala* and *Mission San Fernando* were acquired by the Navy from the Maritime Administration. Renamed *Flagstaff, Johnstown* and *Mussel Shoals* respectively, they were placed under the Instrumentation Ships Project Office by the Navy for use by the National Aeronautics and Space Administration. With the contract for conversion in place at General Dynamics, the ships were again renamed: *Mercury, Redstone* and *Vanguard*. Each ship was modified and enlarged to accommodate the 400 tons of electronics and 210 man crew placed on board. As tracking ships they assisted the Apollo Project for many years throughout the world's oceans.

The *Mission Santa Ynez* would continue her routine of delivering aviation gas and petroleum products. Meanwhile many of her sisters would undergo some very creative and unusual changes.

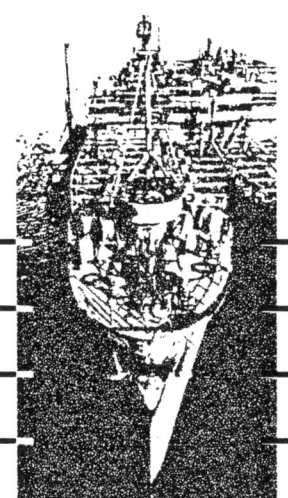

4 MISSIONS IN PIECES

Continuing with the *Mission Santa Ynez* we find that she sailed for Port Arthur, Texas, went through the Panama Canal to San Pedro, California, returned through the Canal (it was her eighth transit) and loaded fuel at Amway Bay, Venezuela. From the summer heat of the tropics on July 9, 1964, the *Ynez* sailed to the barren wastes of Sondrestrom, Greenland, arriving there twelve days later. The ship then ran a three month series of shuttles between the Caribbean and Labrador and Newfoundland.

It was on these runs that the crew was inducted into the Order of the Top of the World. Similar to those ceremonies centered around dateline or equator crossings, seamen who cross the arctic circle are presented certificates for passing that line of demarcation. In part, the certificate reads:

"To all Sailors wherever ye may be; and to all Whale, Seal, Polar Bear, Walrus, Sea Otter, Muskox, Blue Nose Mermaids and other living things of the Polar Seas, Greetings: Know ye that by the grace of His Majesty Boreas Rex, Emperor of the Realm of Eternal Whiteness, Ruler of the Midnight Sun and of the Aurora Borealis, Master of the Howling Gales and of the Ice and Snow, Sovereign of all that lives within the Frozen Wastes:

"On this _____ day of _____ in the year _____ A.D., in Latitude 66 33' N., Longitude _____ the _____ year of MSTS, and the _____ year of the MSTS Arctic Operations was carried on the wings of Boreas across the ARCTIC CIRCLE."

The outside temperature precluded any kind of "crossing the line" ceremony.

The only mishap during this period was that the ship lost her port anchor and three links of chain while moving from anchorage to the dock at St. George's Bay, Newfoundland (Harmon Air Force Base).

In October, 1964 she was taken off that run and operated strictly within the Gulf of Mexico: Beaumont, Lake Charles, Jacksonville, Texas City, and Aruba.

It was while in Aruba on April 30, 1965 that the third assistant engineer was logged for being drunk on watch. He was relieved of duty and fined half a day's pay. His comment recorded in the official log was, "I don't remember being in the Engine Room."

It was a bad year for the engine department. On July 8, the same year, the second assistant engineer had a similar problem. Returning to the ship drunk at three in the morning, he fell asleep with a lighted cigarette in his hand and set his mattress on fire. The captain fined him the cost of the mattress, two pillows, a bed spread, two pillow cases, and the cost of the steward's and messman's overtime involved in putting out the fire and replacing the damaged bedding. The total bill was $64.53.

With the escalation of the conflict in Vietnam there developed a need for the ocean transport of unusually heavy, odd shaped pieces of equipment such as military tanks, generators, airplanes, vehicles and the return of similar pieces of damaged equipment to the United States for repair. As there were not enough ships in existence to fill that need they had to be built. Rather than build them new, it was decided to make them up by converting existing ships. Once again the Mission tankers' adaptability proved its worth. A design was developed for Hudson Waterways Inc. that included two 45 ton capacity derrick cranes servicing a single hatch. Mounted on "flight decks" above the hatch, the cranes serviced not only the inner holds, but the main deck and flight deck as well. These "Seatrains" specialized in heavy and outsized rolling stock. They could, in fact carry train locomotives and cars, having tracks fitted on their decks for such purposes. In addition they carried military vehicles and aircraft which didn't fit on other types of ships.

In 1966 the *Mission San Jose* was renamed *Ohio*. Under that name, the following year it was cut into three sections, with the forepart becoming part of the *Seatrain Maine*, the midbody becoming part of the *Seatrain Washington* and the after section becoming part of the *Seatrain Ohio*.

Because the Mission tankers were powered by turbo-electric engines, they had the ability to be readily converted to electrical power plants — the basic equipment was already there. The fact

Order of the Top of the World

To all Sailors wherever ye may be; and to
all Whale, Seal, Polar Bear, Walrus, Sea Otter, Muskox,
Blue Nose Mermaids and other living things of the Polar Seas

Greetings. Know ye that by grace of His Majesty Boreas Rex, Emperor of the Realm of
Eternal Whiteness, Ruler of the Midnight Sun and of the Aurora Borealis, Master of the
Howling Gales and of the Ice and Snow, Sovereign of all that lives within the Frozen Wastes

_____ day of _____ in the year _____ A.D., in Latitude 66° 33′ N., Longitude _____
_____ year of MSTS, and the _____ year of the MSTS Arctic Operations, was car
reas across the

Arctic Circle

to the gates of the Top of the World; Wherein His Princely Guardian into the Glisnian and
of the Auroral Arctic Empire of His Imperial Majesty having truly tried the intrepid trav
nored trials to wit: Partaking of quak, and of the Nectar of the Gods; and the adding to the
tes by the giving of the heat and moisture of the body; by virtue of the trust placed in him
ty, Boreas Rex, doth welcome this intrepid and honored soul into the Auroral Arctic Empi
e the coveted rights and privileges of his silent realm.

Presented to the crew during the Gulf of Mexico–Greenland shuttle of the
early '60's, the Top of the World certificate is typical of the rare "crossing the
line" traditions of seafaring.

that they carried a relatively high rating of 10,000 horsepower was a plus. Needing power generators in Vietnam, the Army converted two Mission tankers, the *Caney* (laid down as *Mission Los Angeles*) and *Tamalpais* (laid down as *Mission San Francisco*) to floating power plants. The conversion was done by Alabama Shipbuilding and Dry Dock Corporation and the ships placed in Cam Ranh Bay. They were abandoned when the United States left Vietnam.

Meanwhile orders came to the *Mission Santa Ynez* for a run to the South Pacific. Taking on a load of fuel in Los Angeles she sailed for Guam, where she arrived on January 25, 1966. From Guam she sailed to Kwajalein, where another drinking problem occurred.

Shortly after departing Kwajalein, it was discovered that the oiler on the 4 to 8 watch was taking incorrect temperature and pressure readings. He was relieved of duties and demoted to wiper. His comment in the official log was, "I only had one reading wrong."

The following day he was found drunk in his quarters and unable to perform his new duties as wiper. He was fined a day's pay.

The ship arrived at Corpus Christi, Texas on February 23, 1966 followed by Port Arthur on March 7. And yet another incident.

While approaching the Taylor Bayou turning basin, prior to docking at the Gulf Oil Company Terminal, the *Ynez* discovered a dredge working one side of the channel. The pilot signaled the dredge with one blast, which the dredge answered, indicating the ship could pass with the dredge on its port side. As it did so, the vessel hit the corner of the dredge, dropped the starboard anchor, raised it again, and proceeded to the dock. Ringing FWE at 1643, Captain Moretti went below, resigned to another evening of reports and letters.

The remainder of March and the first part of April were spent delivering fuel to American bases at Rota, Cartegena and El Ferrol, Spain. Returning to Lake Charles and Pascagoula, the ship then proceeded to the West Coast. Traveling as far north as Haines, Alaska, where, on Christmas Day, one of the bedroom stewards was logged for being too drunk to work, she then retraced her path to the Gulf.

In October of 1966 the *Mission San Antonio* was converted to the *Seatrain San Juan* by the Savannah Machine and Foundry Company. The following month the same company converted the *Mission San Gabriel* to the *Seatrain Delaware*.

The Mission Santa Ynez waiting for assignment to a loading berth.
V.H. Young

The impetus of Vietnam and developing shipping technology brought about other revolutions in the carriage of cargo. One of these was containers. The lack of internal hull structure made the mission tankers ideal for conversion to container ships. Their hulls could be modified relatively inexpensively and fitted with slots in which to stack containers. The first such conversion of a Mission tanker was the *Mission Carmel*. In 1967 she was rebuilt by Todd Shipyard in Galveston for Sea-Land to become the *Houston*.

Meanwhile the year 1967 saw Seatrain conversions continue apace. The *Mission San Diego* was cut in half with the forepart becoming part of the *Seatrain Ohio* and the after part becoming part of the *Seatrain Washington*. The *Mission Soledad* was converted to become the *Seatrain California* (although two years later she was converted again, this time into a container ship). The *Mission San Luis Obispo* became the *Seatrain Puerto Rico* with the addition of part of the midbody from the *Fruitvale Hills*. A second section of this midbody went into the conversion of the *Mission Santa Barbara* to make up the *Seatrain Carolina*. The two latter conversions were done by Newport News Shipbuilding and Drydock Company.

Arriving at Aransas Pass, Texas on February 20, 1967, the *Mission Santa Ynez* had another spell of "*Ynez* luck." The visibility was eight miles until she entered the breakwater. Out of nowhere a thick fog set in. The next thing the captain knew, his ship was sitting on the bottom, having grounded on the port side of the channel. She came off on the next high tide, after all the ballast water had been pumped off and two tugs were put into play.

In April of 1967 the *Mission San Carlos* was converted to the *Seatrain Maryland* by having the fore and midship section of the *San Jacinto* welded to her after section.

In January of 1968 the *Mission Solano* was converted to a containership by Todd Shipyards Corporation of Galveston and renamed *Jacksonville*.

After a year of servicing her old haunts in the Gulf, the hardworking *Mission Santa Ynez* loaded fuel and sailed for Yokohama. It was May of 1968. Vietnam had become a major conflict.

The *Mission Santa Ynez's* first tour in Vietnam lasted about four months. During that time she delivered fuel from Yokohama (June 6, 1968) to Qui Nhon (June 15, July 7, July 11, July 22, August 18, September 13, and October 5) Cam Ranh Bay (July 9, July 20 and October 3) and Vung Ro (August 13). The only crew problem was one of the oilers (engine department again) who went berserk and had to be repatriated.

Fathometers in the chartroom. These told the story when the Mission Santa Ynez grounded in the fog. Note the trace on the chart at the left rises from the center of the chart almost to the top — indicating rapid shoaling.
Credit the author

It happened while at anchor in Qui Nhon. At three in the morning on July 3, 1968, the first assistant engineer was awakened from a sound sleep by someone pounding on his door. Opening it, he found the oiler from the 12 to 4 watch standing in the passageway.

"The Third Engineer grabbed me and shoved me."

"Why can't you fellows go on and behave yourselves," said the First rubbing the sleep from his eyes and trying to comprehend what was happening.

The oiler left. The first decided to get dressed and find out what was going on. As he finished dressing, the oiler returned.

"The third engineer hit me."

"How many times did the third engineer hit you?"

"Once."

"Did the third engineer hit you in the side?"

"No, it was behind the neck."

The first assistant then woke the chief engineer and the engine department union delegate. They trooped down to the engineroom to quiz the third assistant.

The chief asked the third if he hit the oiler.

"I did not hit the man."

Turning to the oiler, the chief asked if the third had hit him.

"The third knocked me down two times," then turning to the third, he said, "If you stay on this ship, I will kill you! I'll kill you!"

The third asked, "Which was it, one time or two."

"You stay topside more than anyone on the watch, but when I stay up thirty-five minutes you send the second pumpman around looking for me." Turning to the chief he said, "I know what I'm saying. If I have to stay on this watch with him, I'll kill him. I'm not going to even turn the bilge pump off. Now how do you like that?"

To diffuse the situation the first ordered the oiler to call the oncoming 4 to 8 watch.

His response was, "The third hit me three times. I have been wanting a case ever since I was on the ship and now I have it."

Captain Moretti was called at 4 a.m. and investigated the incident. At 8 a.m. he filled out a Masters Certificate of Service (required when sending a seaman ashore in a foreign country to see a doctor) and sent the oiler to the 85th Evacuation Hospital for treatment. At the time he observed, "... no bruises or marks on his face or neck to indicate someone had struck him."

Examination at the hospital revealed no signs of injury, although the crewman was admitted anyway.

With the oiler still in the hospital, the ship sailed for Cam Ranh Bay on July 8. Returning to Qui Nhon on July 12, the man was returned to the vessel.

There were no more problems until July 24 when he refused to work. He told the First, "I'm not going on watch. I'm not working anymore." He was relieved of duty and repatriated to the United States before the ship sailed.

After brief stopovers in Subic Bay and Batangas, Philippine Islands in October of 1968, the tanker returned to San Pedro, California.

On October 10, 1968 the forepart of the *Anacostia AO-94* (laid down as *Mission Alamo*) arrived at Santander for scrapping attached to the afterpart of the *Nautilus*. These were the leftovers from welding the forepart of the *Nautilus* to the afterpart of the *Anacostia* to create the *Penn Ranger* in November of the same year.

In March of 1969 we find the *Santa Ynez* in Beaumont, Texas where she spent most of that year serving by now familiar ports in the Gulf of Mexico.

In November of 1969 the *Mission Dolores* was converted to the containership *Tampa* by Todd Shipyards of Galveston, Texas.

The *Mission San Lorenzo* was stricken from the Navy lists on January 1, 1970. She was deactivated and served out her time as a water-storage hulk in Guantanamo Bay, Cuba.

Following another transit of the Panama Canal, the *Mission Santa Ynez* once again sailed into San Pedro on January 21, 1970.

After a coastwise voyage to San Francisco and Seattle, the dependable ship pointed her bow toward Vietnam. This time there were no crew complications. Months were spent loading and delivering fuel to the ships and ports of Southeast Asia. Qui Nhon, Cam Ranh Bay, Danang and Nha Trang were on the receiving end with Yokohama and Subic Bay serving as the source of supply.

In June of 1971 two mission tankers, the *Mission Santa Cruz* and the *Mission San Rafael* were sold to the Boston Metals Corporation for scrapping. Both ships had spent their earlier years either laid up in the Reserve fleet or working for the navy.

After a year in the Far East, the *Ynez* returned to the West Coast. This time she was put on a milk run that brought her from Kodiak, Alaska, to Ozol, California, to El Segundo, California, to Haines, Alaska, to Point Molate, San Francisco, Richmond and Rodeo in the San Francisco Bay area, thence Whittier, Alaska, and finally Adak, Alaska. Spending the months of November and December, 1971 on this run gave the crew a break from the heat and anxiety of Vietnam.

It was only a short respite, for the conflict in Southeast Asia intensified. From Adak, the *Ynez* sailed for Yokohama arriving there 9 days out on the 18th of December, 1971. Christmas Day was spent in Sasebo, Japan and the 28th in Subic Bay, Philippine Islands. The New Year was rung in, or shot in, at Cam Ranh Bay.

The navy oiler *Pasig AO-91* (laid down as the *Mission San Xavier*) entered the Suisun Bay Reserve Fleet in 1972. At the same time the *Mission Buenaventura* was stricken from the Navy lists and the *Mission Santa Maria* was sold for scrap at Split. The latter ship bore the distinction of having the most varied career of the Mission tankers. Undergoing ten name changes and sailing under the flags of eight nations, she was modified twice, once by being lengthened and once by being converted to an off-shore well-drilling tender.

From Cam Ranh, the *Ynez* began a coastal shuttle service of that war-torn country that lasted a full 23 months. At first several days were spent in each port: Qui Nhon, Nha Trang, Vung Tau, Danang and China Beach. But, as the conflict intensified, it became safer to leave port each night and sail at reduced speed or sometimes just drift at sea, until morning when the ship returned to the same port or sometimes the next one on the itinerary.

In October of 1972 the *Mission San Luis Rey* was sold from the Beaumont Reserve Fleet to shipbreakers in Cleveland, Ohio.

It was November, 1972 before the *Mission Santa Ynez* left the war zone, this time for good. Sailing from Danang on November 17, she arrived in Sasebo, Japan on the 24th. From Sasebo she sailed for Pohang, Korea, where misadventure struck again.

Carrying a load of 11,000 long tons of refined petroleum, the ship was maneuvering into a set of fixed mooring lines coming from shore. The tug *527* was to assist by pushing the stern around within reach of the mooring cables. With a twenty knot northwesterly wind and a five foot northwesterly swell, the tug pushed when she should have pulled or the perhaps tugmaster was over-zealous or maybe the local pilot, Captain Kim, gave the wrong command. Regardless of the cause, the result was a large dent, administered by the bow of the tug to the hull plating of the *Mission Santa Ynez*. Fortunately there was no loss of cargo and no injuries.

Next came a shuttle of the Far East that lasted until February of 1973. Yokohama was the next port after Pohang, then Kaoshiung, Taiwan; Chin Wan, Okinawa; Sasebo, Pohang, Sasebo, Pohang, Chin Wan, Buckner Bay, Okinawa; Sattahip, Thailand; Bangkok, Thailand; Sasebo, Pohang and finally Pusan,

In San Francisco Bay with a full load of fuel, 1973.
Courtesy George Lamuth

Korea. She arrived at Los Angeles on February 22, 1973, twenty days out from Pusan.

For the next two years the *Mission Santa Ynez* went coastwise from California to Alaska and Hawaii. Tankers often find themselves at unusual ports in addition to the normal ones that other ships use. The routine ports for the ship during this period were Long Beach, San Francisco, Seattle and Adak. The unusual ones were Cherry Point, Ozol, Kodiak, Whittier, Nikiski, Manchester, Stockton, Oleum, Mukilteo, Wilmington, Portland, Anacortes, Mulate, Estero Bay, El Segundo, Port Angeles, Kwajalein, Barber's Point, Pearl Harbor and Ferndale. Just knowing where these places are gave the crew a background in local geography equal to that of many college students.

On January 13, 1975 the tired, overworked, but ever willing ship arrived in San Francisco for the last time. After almost 30 years of continuous service, misadventures and rough usage, she was worn out. She entered the Reserve Fleet in Suisun Bay on March 6, 1975, proudly holding the record, despite all her mishaps, of the longest service to Military Sealift Transport Service of any ship of her class.

On September 29, 1975 the *Mission Loreto* left the Suisun Bay Reserve fleet for the scrappers. She was followed on November 12 by the *Pasig (Mission San Xavier)*.

On January 2, 1976 the *Mission Los Angeles* departed the James River Reserve Fleet for the shipbreakers. Four days later on the other side of the continent, the *Mission Santa Ana* (laid down as *Concho AO-102*) departed the Suisun Bay Reserve Fleet for the same purpose. She was sold to National Metal and Steel, a West Coast ship dismantler. She was followed by the *Mission Purisima* on May 11. Sold to American Ship Dismantlers, she left Suisun Bay and was quickly converted to scrap. In 1982 the *Soubarissen AO-94* (laid down as the *Mission Santa Ana*) was sold out of the Beaumont Reserve Fleet to Brownsville Steel and Salvage for scrapping.

After her many years of knock-about service, drunken crewmembers and lack of recognition, the *Ynez* finally achieved a distinction. Of the thirty-four Mission ships, *Mission Santa Ynez* was now the sole survivor — the last Mission tanker. A year later she would be given recognition that had eluded her for all her years. It would happen in the most unlikely of places, the backwaters of the National Defense Reserve Fleet at Suisun Bay.

When the Mission Santa Ynez came to the Reserve Fleet, one of the crew left a sentimental message. He was fond of "the old girl."
Credit the author

Answering the call one last time, the vessel was taken out for current tests.
Courtesy George Lamuth

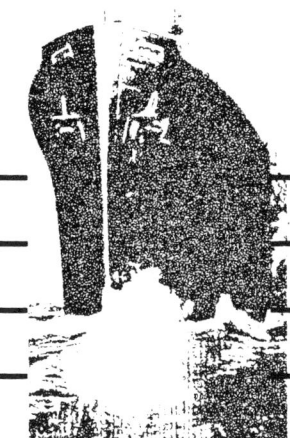

5
THE FINAL MISSION

The last Mission tanker briefly answered the call one more time in August of 1983. The US Navy took her out for a week to serve as a test platform for the analysis of the effects of current on a ship in the Carquinez Straits. Under empty and loaded conditions she responded enthusiastically to current and stress gauges, then returned to the fleet on August 14, 1983 to await her last voyage, presumably at the end of a towline en route to the breaker's torch.

But her story may continue. The Sausalito Historical Society established the Marinship Museum to commemorate a proud chapter in Sausalito's history. Located in the Army Corps of Engineers' Bay Model building, the museum is on the site of the old Marinship Corporation yard. Unknown to the curators as they developed the museum exhibits, the last of the ships built at Marinship was only a few miles away riding at anchor waiting to be scrapped. In early 1988, by fortunate happenstance, they became aware of her existence. Quickly a plan was developed to loan her to the museum for a few weeks. When and if that happens she will be the only ship in the world ever to return to the exact place she was built and launched. An alternative plan calls for the ship to be permanently moored alongside the museum. A further alternative is to mount major parts of the wheelhouse and engine room as permanent exhibits in the Marinship Museum.

The *Mission Santa Ynez*'s career has been one of dogged persistence and long suffering endurance. It is hoped she, or at least parts of her, can stay there as an inspiring example of American know-how, ingenuity and skill. Because, despite all the dents, bumps, torn rails, scraped sides and drunken crew members, she stands as a symbol, the last of a proud line that overcame the odds and did what she was built to do. Perhaps it was her challenge all along to finally triumph over adversity to become the last Mission tanker.

"There is a port of no return, where ships
May ride at anchor for a little space
And then, some starless night, the cable slips,
Leaving an eddy at the mooring place ...
Gulls, veer no longer. Sailor, rest your oar.
No tangled wreckage will be washed ashore.

Leslie Nelson Jennings

The Mission Santa Ynez *looking ghost-like as she sits at the Reserve Fleet in 1989.*
Credit the author

Bibliography

Engle, Eloise and Arnold S. Lott.
America's Maritime Heritage.
Annapolis: Naval Institute Press, 1977.

Kennedy, Don H.
Ship Names.
Charlottesville: The University Press of Virginia, 1974.

La Dage, John.
Merchant Ships.
Cambridge: Cornell Maritime Press, 1955.

Martin, J.H. and Geoffry Bennett.
Pictorial History of Ships.
Secaucus: Chartwell Books, Inc., 1977.

Sawyer, L.A. and W.H. Mitchell.
Victory Ships and Tankers.
London: David Charles: Newton Abbot, 1974.

United States Dept. of the Navy.
The Dictionary of American Naval Fighting Ships.
Washington: GPO, 1976.

Index of Ships

Abatan 26
Anacostia 26,69
Caney 26,64
USS Chukawan 50,52
Concho 26,72
Conecuh 26
Contocook 26
Corvallis 22,24
Cosmic 46
Elna II 46
Flagstaff 60
Fruitvale Hills 66
Houston 66
Jacksonville 66
Johnstown 60
LT-648 48
Mercury 60
USS Missinewa 50
Mission Alamo 26,69
Mission Buenaventura . 26,70
Mission Capistrano . . . 26,52
Mission Carmel 26,66
Mission De Pala 26,60
Mission Dolores 26,69
Mission Loreto 26,50,72
Mission Los Angeles . . . 26,48,64,72
Mission Purisima 24,48,72
Mission San Antonio . . 26,64
Mission San Carlos 26,66
Mission San Diego 26,66
Mission San Fernando . 26,60
Mission San Francisco . 26,46,48,64
Mission San Gabriel . . . 26,64
Mission San Jose 24,62
Mission San Juan 24,60
Mission San Lorenzo . . 26,69
Mission San Luis Obispo 26,66
Mission San Luis Rey . . 26,70
Mission San Miguel . . . 24,48
Mission San Rafael 26,69
Mission San Xavier 26,70,72
Mission Santa Ana 26,45,48,72
Mission Santa Barbara . 24,26,66
Mission Santa Clara . . . 26,58
Mission Santa Cruz 24,69
Mission Santa Maria . . . 26,70
Mission Santa Ynez 12,14,19,
    20,22,24,26,31,32,33,34,36,
    38,42,44,5,46,48,50,52,54,56,
    58,60,61,64,6,69,70,72,75
Mission Solano 26,66
Mission Soledad 26,66
Mussel Shoals 60
Nautilus 69
Ohio 62
Pasig 26,70,72
Penn Ranger 69
Plattsburg 38
Redstone 60
San Jacinto 66
Seatrain California 66
Seatrain Carolina 66
Seatrain Delaware 64
Seatrain Maine 62
Seatrain Maryland 66
Seatrain Ohio 62,66
Seatrain Puerto Rico . . . 66
Seatrain San Juan 64
Seatrain Washington . . . 62,66
Soubarissen 26,45,72
Tamalpais 26,64
Tampa 69
Vanguard 60
USS Waccamaw 50
USS Yosemite 56,58